MENDING
BROKENNESS

MENDING BROKENNESS

A spiritual journey to authentic wholeness

Sabrina B. Gray

XULON PRESS

Xulon Press
2301 Lucien Way #415
Maitland, FL 32751
407.339.4217
www.xulonpress.com

Paperback ISBN-13: 978-1-66283-767-8
Ebook ISBN-13: 978-1-66283-768-5

✳ ✳ ✳

My first book is dedicated to

The One who taught me how to dance through life while listening to His music, Jesus the Christ, my best friend, my lover and my confidante.

To Billy Graham for sharing the gift of salvation with me when I attended his crusade in 1964 at the baseball stadium in Kansas City, Missouri, and accepted Christ as my Savior at eight years of age.

To my mother, Clydia M. Turner, in taking her child to the crusade and taught me so many things through her life. I am grateful for the nuggets of wisdom from her I still use and pass on to others.

✳ ✳ ✳

TABLE OF CONTENTS

✴ ✴ ✴

In this fantastic book, "Mending Brokenness", Sabrina holds nothing back in sharing how God taught her to straighten her back and boldly walk upright through each day using His strength as a walking stick. How do I know? Because I am her husband and see her standing against the fierce storms of life.

"Mending Brokenness" is for everyone because brokenness whispers in our ears, "You will never be able to put yourself back together again"; but with God's strength and this book...YOU WILL!

Buy two copies of this book; one for yourself and one for somebody struggling with brokenness in her/his life.

Robert "Bob" Gray
Husband
Assistant Pastor of Bethel AME Church
Boston, MA
Boston Celtic Chaplain
futureyouwantnow.com

 ✴ ✴ ✴

ACKNOWLEDGMENTS

WHENEVER I READ a book, I always read the acknowledgements because I like to know who was behind the scenes helping the author. I could not have written this book without the direction, encouragement, and inspiration I received from so many people.

First, to my husband of twenty years, Bob Gray. You have taught me so many things just by the way you live your life, and I have had some of my best laughs from your humor. You have inspired me to be steadfast with my writing, because I have watched you labor in the publication of your second book, *Decide to Become Awesome*, which has become a bestseller. But most of all, I am awestruck with your spirit of servitude. You serve me and so many others with an attitude and heart of service. There is nothing like Bob Gray's love for me that sees, tells, and supports me like no one else. Love you and thank you!

To Gigi Green, who I first suggested we co-author a book together because we both had experienced so many similar things. I dropped the ball, but she went on to write her life story in a best-selling book, *My Life*. She continues to encourage and push me. Thank you, Sis G!

To my friend of forty-plus years, Paulea Elizabeth Mooney-McCoy. You will never know how much I cherish your unconditional love and acceptance; two things I have needed that you always gave with no strings attached. Thank you for your insightful editing notes and suggestions. You are my BFF.

To Rev. Viola P. Morris Buchanan, the editor of the *HULL*, The African Methodist Episcopal Boston-Hartford District Christian Education Newsletter, who offered me space to write five articles in the *HULL*'s electronic newsletter. Your go-ahead to submit the articles was a confirmation for this book, and those articles became the first five chapters of this book. Thank you!

To Arleigh Prelow, my Wollaston Beach walking-and-talking buddy. You always have such encouraging words, creative ideas and professional editing remarks. I depend on and lean on your support. Thank you for the gentle pushes.

To the late Al Tyson and Joyce Simms-Tyson, my honest and steadfast friends, mentors, and restaurant connoisseurs. Thank you for your valuable suggestions and always opening your home for me to visit and eat.

To Stephanie Martin, my new writing buddy. When I reminded you to keep writing, I had to continue as well. Thank you for your editing notes.

To Ashley Zak Kimble, my Orlando writing friend. When I first accepted the call to write this book, you were the first person I publicly shared this with, and we have developed a writing camaraderie and encourage each other to...just write!

Acknowledgments

To my pastors and the founders of Bethel AME Church in Boston, Massachusetts, Ray Hammond and Gloria White-Hammond, who were my friends before they were my pastors. Your friendship, conversations, and sermons have contributed greatly to this book.

And lastly, to Jesus Christ, because I strive to put You on a track all by Yourself, not competing with anyone or anything. Without Your help to see You in everything, my life would have no meaning. I can't wait to see You face to face—the One who was and is always there; who always loves me and wants the best for me. I love you, Lord God. You are my Brokenness-Mender and the reason I am writing this book. To You be the glory!

I.H.T.W.N.
Introduction

WHY WRITE ABOUT BROKENNESS?

"GOOD WRITING REQUIRES courage—first to give voice to the truth...embracing vulnerability could unlock important doors for writing." [1] I have a voice, and I have something to say; and through this, I embrace vulnerability in my writing.

My writing journey prayer is:

Lord, teach me how to write creatively, authentically, truthfully, and transparently. Help me express my thoughts, struggles, lessons learned, and growth in words and ways that will resonate with people, so they can grow and be encouraged to walk closer with You. Lord, guide me to be transparent and put myself in vulnerable places as I share through writing. I want to expose my good, bad, and ugly places (uglies), because I am secure in my relationship with You. I can share and confess my uglies because I know I have been forgiven. Lord, I have died to my brokenness, releasing to You all my selfish thoughts, wrong motives, jealousies, and broken ways and responses. Therefore, I can be transparent about the process because brokenness no longer has a hold on me. I am no longer held in its bondage and am free to share painful points, jealousy jewels, and hateful hinderances. There is a freedom, a real release in my spirit...no shame or guilt. Because I can be unapologetically honest with You, I can share freely with others. Amen!

I have to write now (I.H.T.W.N.)- to present God as the One whose love is greater than anything we have ever felt or experienced. It is eternal. I write to encourage people to be honest with God (He can handle it) and themselves and either enter or continue a personal relationship with God through His Son, Jesus. This relationship will inspire them to read, grow, and fall more in love with our God!

I have to write. There is no other option for me in this season of my life. Plus...I have a lot to say. When I was about six years old, I remember writing and illustrating a book titled *The Little Brown Jug*. And as I sat at my mother's feet, I looked up and told her, "Momma, one day I am going to be a writer." That was over fifty years ago, and a whole lot has transpired in my life (not to worry—all fifty years are not in this book). I have walked with the Lord for over fifty years. Therefore, coupled with the need and desire to write and share, I also have a wealth of experience to pull from.

So, how did I come up with the topic of brokenness? Back in 2011, God pressed on me to begin developing a ministry called Kingdom Building Ministries. He directed me to five specific areas to focus on in helping to build His kingdom. These five areas together are like the mosaic tapestry of how God has moved in my life, how I have learned, and how my relationship with Him has developed over the years, each with its own color, landscape, and story.

The first area is: "Train up a child." One of my gifts is teaching, and in the future, I will tell the story of how I grew into my call and vocation of teaching. Within this call, God gave me the vision/dream of opening my own school, which I did 1986-1996 with a good friend, Delores Mitchell. Through Cornerstone Christian Preparatory School, we were able to educate our own children as well as children in various communities from kindergarten through fifth grade.

The second area is this book.* I have had some very broken experiences in my life, and God has instructed me to share these tough, broken places to show that He is the God of brokenness who can, and will, mend us to wholeness. And so, I share my journey from brokenness to wholeness with you, the reader. *Mending Brokenness* is truly my story. Every once in a while we get the chance to change a broken world with our writing. This is my chance.

*The other three areas of kingdom-building ministry will be revealed in my future publications.

"I could feel the sadness in her eyes."
Carlene Bacchus
Friend and prayer partner

Chapter One

DANCING WITH BROKENNESS

MY CHILDHOOD DREAM of marriage quickly became a nightmare when I received an unexpected letter in the mail asking for a divorce. In that moment, I experienced hopelessness, helplessness, and emptiness. I felt hurt, angry, confused, and rejected all at the same time, and was truly broken.

Brokenness is not in the top five or ten topics people would choose to discuss, nor would it be a favorite book selection, which is the reason I have chosen to discuss it. As disciples of Christ, we sometimes omit teachings and discussions on the realization, acceptance, and acknowledgement of our brokenness, instead choosing to blame our brokenness on lack of faith or sin. It is my hope that after reading this book, discussing brokenness will become more than just one of your top choices of topics, but will actually become a tool to help you grow more intimate with our God. My urgent desire is for us to be so close to God that we will embody everything He has empowered us with to make a difference in the building of His kingdom.

When we think of brokenness, words like busted, fractured, shattered, not together, in pieces, not whole, or unglued come to mind. These same synonyms for brokenness can be used to describe broken periods, areas, or events in our lives. We can all recall times when things fell apart; when we didn't have answers; when we had nothing left; when we needed someone to step in because someone had stepped out. We needed someone to save us because we were broken people.

Each of us has experienced some form of brokenness in our lives, large or small (if you haven't, just keep living.) Brokenness can result from a decision we made or something out of our control. It can stem from events from our childhood, loss of a job, failure at school, a failed marriage, or something someone said or did that had devastating consequences. Whatever the catalyst, what distinguishes the results is that our usual "bounce back" is not there; in fact, there is no bounce at all. We are just…broken.

Even in the hopelessness and confusion of my divorce, a situation I thought would leave me disarrayed forever, God mended me. As strange as it may sound, through my brokenness, I became stronger. So, brokenness, can be good! Is that an oxymoron or what? How can life-altering brokenness be good?

First, we must realize we are broken; this is a big, first step. Many people think admitting they are broken and need mending, is a sign of weakness. Not at all, especially with God as the Mender; "those who know they can't do it on their own are the ones who receive God's grace." [2]

In realizing our brokenness, we accept that something ain't quite right. Using swimming as an analogy, our brokenness is like being in deep waters and not knowing how to tread water. As much as we may try, the "brokenness waters" continue to overwhelm us each time we seem to get our heads above the water level. And if that was not unnerving enough, there is an undercurrent of "self-debasement" pulling us too. We tell ourselves, "Something must be wrong with me," and self-talk ourselves into becoming the culprit of blame for our brokenness. Now, I am not the greatest swimmer, and these "waters" can seem quite daunting and treacherous, but we must not allow the realization of our brokenness to lead us to self-debasement and blame. Brokenness can be good and lead to a path of strength and empowerment.

Although we all are broken people to some degree, some of us acknowledge it, while some don't. Some people have learned to live with their brokenness, justifying it with, "This is just who I am,"; "This is just my lot in life,"; or "I can't do any better." So, then they self-medicate because being broken can be painful. Ooooops, did I mention that brokenness hurts?

When we are broken, we hurt emotionally, psychologically, and spiritually: our hearts are wounded. We self-medicate to deal with the pain, using "medicines" like emotional eating, drugs, sex, spending money, or drinking. We do all this trying to fix the brokenness that only One can fix. Only One can mend our brokenness, and that is Jesus.

Jesus is the Mender. He mended me. In the midst of my divorce turmoil, Jesus told me not to deny any of my emotions, but to DANCE with each one. When I felt anger, I danced with it, accepting and embracing that feeling. It was through dancing and embracing what I would normally avoid that I became whole and unbroken with new strength. Jesus restored my hope, replaced my victimization thinking with victory, and filled my emptiness, mending me from brokenness to wholeness.

Oswald Chambers said, "...at the point of despair {brokenness}, we are willing to come to {Jesus} as paupers to receive from Him." [3] Jesus knows each of us personally when we accept Him as our Savior/Mender. He does not berate or make us feel stupid when we are broken, and does not condemn us or make us feel inadequate because of our brokenness. "There is now therefore no condemnation to them which are in Christ Jesus, who walk not after the flesh, but the Spirit," (Rom. 8:1, KJV).

Jesus will love us, even in our brokenness and will graciously begin and continue the process of mending, healing, and delivering until it is completed. "Being confident of this very thing, that he who hath begun a good work in you will perform it until the day of Jesus Christ," (Phil. 1:6 KJV).

God has begun a great work in us and will be faithful to complete it. We need to realize, acknowledge, and accept our brokenness without self-blame, and then turn to the Master Mender to be made whole.

Notes

"As mom's oldest, I remembered a lot from the time of the divorce and the pain I could sense from her as her daughter. She's a true inspiration and role model of someone who has and continues to stand firm in her faith in Jesus, she loves hard, and is able to share her growth with others. I'm proud to be her daughter and to see who she is today despite what she went through."

Rachel Nicole
Oldest daughter of the author
An Educational and Life Consultant

Chapter Two

VICTORY IN VULNERABILITY

ONE THING MY mother taught me when I was young is that honesty is always the best policy.

Dancing with my brokenness meant I had to be honest with God and myself; it was a necessary part of my mending journey. Honesty with God first begins with being honest with ourselves. I had to admit there was sadness, loathing, broken-heartedness, and depression in me, and this required examining uncomfortable and ugly places. When we open our emotions and are honest with ourselves, we allow ourselves to be vulnerable.

Being vulnerable means easily hurt or harmed physically, mentally, or emotionally; being exposed, open, "capable of being physically or emotionally wounded" [4] (Whoever wants this, raise your hand!) Who likes pain? (I see no hands!). Sometimes the peace we seek and need comes through purging our pain, but there is good news! (You really need some after reading that definition!) "I have told you these things, so that in me you may have peace. In this world you will have trouble. But take heart! I have overcome the world." (Jn 16:33 NIV).

All these buzz words—vulnerability, brokenness, and naked-ness—can represent many places we find ourselves in life; places we do not want to go, talk about, reveal, or even admit to ourselves. We all have that one "closet" in our lives we have locked up and thrown away the key. That closet holds the trash of our pain, dirt from our past, and pieces of our brokenness, and behind its door lies hideous, hidden hurts. We must acknowledge the closet and throw open its door, allowing God to come in, dig through, discard, and clean it out. In essence, we have to let God deal with all the stuff we have pushed aside, omitted, ignored, suppressed, denied, and hidden. We can live our lives "skipping around the mulberry bush," but at some point, we need to stop long enough for our "bush" to be pruned for new growth.

Brene Brown, American professor, lecturer, podcast host and author, in her New York Times bestseller titled, *Rising Strong,* writes about the courage to open up, "to bear witness to the human potential for transformation through vulnerability, courage and teaching." [5] In her book, she encourages us to "own our own stories…owning our brokenness with a willingness to revisit, challenge and check our narratives." [6] Owning our own stories needs to include not only our cute childhood memories and life accomplishments but the things in our life closets.

When we open ourselves to God, we do not have to worry about being harmed or wounded. The more I opened up, the more I learned to trust Him with the raw areas of my life. He lovingly took me to my closet and began helping me clean it out—sometimes slowly and gently; other times firmly decluttering and throwing out unwanted contents. When we open ourselves up to Him honestly, He will begin pulling out the stuff we would rather not deal with or pretend we have forgotten. Opening ourselves before God, exposing those hidden and often denied places to Him, is true freedom and release.

Being vulnerable before God was a difficult process for me, but one that became easier. It was difficult because I had to trust the One who had allowed my pain to happen. My "spiritual defenses" rose up big time, and I found it hard to trust God and started trying to do stuff on my own. This is where God was so wonderful. He kept loving, guiding, protecting, and providing for me, never leaving my side, even when I did not want to walk by His side. Oh, I still went to church, sang, prayed, and even went through the Sunday morning rituals. But in my prayer times, when I was alone with Him, He helped me actually let my guard down.

I was so mixed and messed-up emotionally and was angry with everybody (including God). I did not want to be bothered with people (nor God) and blamed God (I had to blame someone). But then I realized I could not feel that way about the One who was still right there with me through it all, still loving me even through my ugliness. I remembered Romans 8:38-39 that lists everything that cannot and will not separate us from His love, in essence nothing—not brokenness, not hurts, not denials. Bit by bit, He began to teach me my new dance, and with each move, I was rebuilding, growing stronger, and loving my journey of transformation. Do you get my drift? I was in a place where He showed me that even in my vulnerability, He still loved and accepted me. I gained victory as I became vulnerable with God. "Vulnerability before God is a safe place. It is the first step in growing in faith" (Journeying with Jesus Lent Devotion).[7]

Whatever your brokenness is, fight for that place of surrender through vulnerability. Fight for it! Satan will try to turn you upside down and inside out with doubt, blame, shame, bitterness, and depression. He will find your weak link and prey on it. Dr. Wanda Turner, a nationally acclaimed Minister, Teacher, Prophet, Life Coach and Best-Selling author shared, "God wants to do a new thing in our old {broken} lives and we must push, press, run, walk, crawl, do whatever we have to" [8] to get to where Jesus died for us to be. Part of our surrender in brokenness requires us to be vulnerable before God. We must own our stories of brokenness, acknowledging and confessing them. Through vulnerability and dancing with our brokenness, God wants to and will love us with His everlasting love. There IS victory in vulnerability with our God!

Notes

※ ※ ※

"Sabrina has been my treasured friend for over forty years and I have witnessed firsthand how she has faced her own seasons of brokenness with courage and hope. These experiences were the fertile ground that God used to grow the wisdom and insights that are in *Mending Brokenness*. This book gives people the permission to admit their brokenness, the courage to enter into the process of healing, and the hope that there is a loving God who has the power to mend the torn pieces of our lives. Sabrina tells of how she felt directed to write this book. We are all thankful that she heeded the prompting of the Spirit."

Rev. Paulea Mooney-McCoy
Dear friend
Ordained Minister
Spiritual Mentor
Educator
Program Developer

※ ※ ※

Chapter Three

FORGIVENESS IS LIKE AN ONION

ONIONS—SLICED, DICED, SIZZLED, or fried---, their sight or smell can elicit a variety of responses. Mouths can begin to salivate awaiting the first taste of a dish ordered with onions. Faces can wrinkle in disgust at the sight or smell of onions, with requests made to "Hold the onions, please!"

Forgiveness is actually like an onion, even though this image may not be what pops into our heads when we think of forgiveness. Forgiveness has layers, and it can stink, but it's part of the mending path for transforming our brokenness and helps us gain victory when we express our vulnerable pains and hurts to God. God forgives, so we can too. We have a choice to forgive just as we have been forgiven.

Have you ever forgiven someone (or thought you had), and then he or she does or says something that sends you back to those unforgiving thoughts and places? I have!

A family member psychologically and emotionally hurt me badly when I was a child. The hurt and pain caused me to be repulsed at the sight of this person, and retched memories constantly haunted me. God did not judge or condemn me for my repulsive thoughts. Instead, He told me I needed to confront the person and reveal the pain that was caused. Now, did I run out and have this confrontation? No. I had to work through some things myself first, like being willing to forgive and to let the person off "my revenge hook." It took me some time, and God reminded me lovingly, yet firmly, that I needed to go and confront the person in love without hatred or bitterness. God understood my feelings, and when I tried to justify them, He reminded me how He had forgiven me when I did not deserve it, so I needed to confront the person, share the pain that I had experienced, and forgive. To do this, I had to travel a distance. (God really has a sense of humor. I had to spend money to go to someone who had hurt me!).

I reluctantly called and decided to meet with this person. Praise God, when we met, we were able to talk honestly, confess, cry, and forgive. Forgiveness was done! Hallelujah! But six months later, this person said things to me that took me right back to that repulsive, unforgiven space. Wait, God, what happened? We confessed, cried, expressed our love, and forgave. What's going on? That's when God told me that forgiveness is like an onion; it has layers. I had forgiven this person, but the manifestation would be in layers, like an onion, a continual process. I would forgive at each layer, each time something resurfaced. And each time I did, the forgiveness would become more solid and sustainable. The Holy Spirit directs us to forgive, and the process starts in our hearts. Victoria Osteen, American author and co-pastor of Lakewood Church in Houston, Texas, explains in her book, *Love Your Life*, "Forgiveness is more than just words, it's a heart attitude that induces spiritual transformation." She goes on to explain, "Our hearts become clean through the power of forgiveness." [9] The heart's attitude is a part of the process of forgiveness.

Forgiveness is the letting go of offenses, and the letting go may be a continual process. In our spirits, we may have forgiven, but our mind and actions sometimes have to catch up. Forgiveness is immediate, but the emotional healing and maintaining forgiveness is a journey. True and total forgiveness involves the heart, mind, will, and emotions.

Like an onion, forgiveness can sometimes "stink." It stinks because we don't want to forgive the offender. We don't always feel like, or even believe, we should forgive. It's true that what someone did or said may have truly been unforgivable. But, "Forgiveness is setting the prisoner free and realizing the prisoner is you." [10] We choose freedom when we choose to forgive.

When the process is really stinking, remember that forgiveness is for your freedom in God, not the offender's. Forgiveness may seem like you are letting the offender off the hook, but it is actually releasing you. When we forgive, we release our right to take revenge and give it over to God. "Do not take revenge, my friends, but leave room for God's wrath, for it is written: 'It's mine to avenge; I will repay,' says the Lord" (Rom. 12:9, NIV). Even when forgiving someone seems unfair, God is always fair, and we have the God-given ability to forgive just as He did.

Forgiveness is a choice. Just like we can choose to have onions on our burger or order a salad without onions, we can choose to forgive or not. But if we decide not to forgive, it is a costly choice. By choosing to forgive we receive freedom and strengthen our relationship with God. By choosing not to forgive, we block God's blessings and hinder our relationship with Him. We cannot walk in the light of Christ when we have not forgiven, and we grieve the Holy Spirit when we harbor unforgiveness. There is bondage in unforgiveness. "Stand fast therefore in the liberty [freedom] wherewith Christ hath made us free and be not entangled again with the yoke of bondage" (Gal. 5:1, KJV).

There is no quick fix for devastating pains and hurts afflicted by others. The danger is in not acknowledging that we have suppressed and hidden unforgiveness toward someone in our closet. Let our goal be to resurrect, recognize, and release the brokenness unforgiveness can perpetrate. Choose today to unearth any unforgiveness you may have. Don't let the "steel shackles of anger, bitterness and even hatred of unforgiveness chain us to the offense and offender." [11] John Neider, Radio Host, Teacher and Author and the late Thomas M. Thompson, journalist and author, offer three decisions we need to make to forgive:

1) Trust God's Word---Drop your preconceived ideas about forgiveness and be open to what God has to say. This is God's domain.

2) Allow the Holy Spirit to be your counselor---He will reveal to you the persons you need to forgive and give you the ability to follow through.

3) Expect God to do a special work in you---God does not want you to live your life tied up in knots. He wants to set you free from the prison of your personal pain. Forgiveness is your choice. We have been forgiven to forgive. Choose to serve your forgiveness with onions.

Forgiveness is Like an Onion

<u>Notes</u>

17

"Thank you so much for allowing me to enter into your life through your book, *Mending Brokenness*. You were your authentic self. Your vulnerability portrayed your strength throughout your journey. I thank you for sharing this raw and personal perspective. Your faith is inspirational and contagious-you have strengthened my own faith through your words and actions. As we discussed, we are all broken and with God's love we can embrace this as part of who we are and move forward with God's guidance."

Susan DeSanto-Madeya, PhD, RN, FAAN
Miriam Weyker Endowed Chair for
Palliative Care/ Associate Professor
University of Rhode Island,
College of Nursing

Chapter Four

STORMS VERSUS SUFFERING

ARE STORMS AND suffering the same thing, and does their purposes equate their meanings? Are storms forms of suffering, or is suffering a type of storm? Storms and suffering can be part of our brokenness but are most likely not one of our favorite subjects to think about or experience! Nevertheless, they are a part of all Christians' journeys, and they glorify God and strengthen us.

I offer that if we understand the mending process, when storms rage in our lives or we slip into suffering, we will be able to yield, dance, or swim through troubled waters better.

Many times, when we witness and invite others to have saving faith in Jesus, we neglect to tell them the reality of Christianity. We like to tell people about Christ's grace, love, forgiveness, and making a way out of no way. It's important to tell people all these wonderful promises, but we need to include the hard-time promises too so that when they encounter difficult times (and they will), they will know the promises of God are guaranteed.

One of the questions I wrestled with was if suffering, storms, and tribulations are distinguished by the amount of time spent in each one—for example, if storms are short, difficult experiences while suffering takes place over a longer period of time? Also, are tribulations bumps in the road, like getting a flat tire or missing a flight, or something more serious like getting laid off or being passed over for a promotion? Let's consider Job. For Job, things went from bad to worse. Would we call Job's suffering a bunch of storms and tribulations?

Another question I wrestled with was if people determine the length of their suffering by their response and willingness to yield—i.e., does disobedience or stubbornness affect suffering? Obedience frees us. The Word says, "Good understanding wins favor, but the way of transgressors is hard" (Prov. 13:14, KJV). It also says, "In this world we will have tribulations" (Jn 16:33a, KJV).

My storm was my divorce. As I sat in the divorce court room, I could not believe my eternal bliss of marriage was ending. There was plenty of thunder booms of disbelief and shocking lightning bolts as the reality of my broken dream rained tears of dismay down on me. The suffering I experienced was difficult, as I also had to face helping my five children understand and make sense of this torrential storm. There is a necessary link between suffering and glory (Eliot, 1990). [12] "...and that my momentary troubles are producing for me an eternal glory that far outweighs them all, as I keep my eyes focused on You" (Myers, 1994). [13]

So, how do we endure storms and suffering? One of my favorite songs I listened to during my divorce time was Yolanda Adams's "Through the Storm." [14] The chorus says:

> While riding through the storm, Jesus holds me
> in His arms, I am not afraid of the stormy winds
> and waves, Though the tides become high, He
> holds me while I ride, I find safety in His arms,
> while riding through the storm, I have no fear of
> the raging seas, Knowing Jesus is there for me,
> He can speak to the winds and the waves and
> make them behave. (3)

The answer is in one word, and that is RIDE. Ride through your storm. Don't fight through it, don't ignore it, and don't try to do it yourself; rather, ride your storm with Jesus in the safety of His arms. Think about a roller coaster. As it goes up and down, around curves, dipping and swaying, you ride as the car moves along its given path until it comes to a stop. The same applies to our storms and suffering. We ride them with Jesus. I rode with Jesus through the pain and learned to share my experience without shame, and received redemption each time I shared. I opened myself to God and allowed Him to use what I had experienced to heal and help others. "The undergirding conviction is God, Himself, He is the Answer. What we all need in tough times, tribulations and suffering is an intimate, healing experience of His grace and goodness, peace and power" (Olgive, 1982). [15]

Ruth Meyer encourages us to see our trials as friends rather than intruders. "In spite of what I think or feel when I get my eyes off You, I choose not to resist my trials as intruders, but to "welcome them as friends" (Myers, 1994) [16]. "We must dwell in Him-abide, remain, make our home in,--stay---sharing His life, drawing His strength." (Eliot, 1990). [17]

As we face our storms or experience suffering, let us remember His mercies are new every morning and be at peace because Christ overcame: and with Him, we can too. Don't give Satan any brownie points by becoming bitter, depressed, or stubborn. Understand that God sees and knows what you are experiencing. His promise to never leave or forsake us is good, even during storms and suffering. He is not standing on the side observing; it is in those times we do not see our footprints in the sand that He is carrying us. [18] It may not be nice or comfortable. It may be painful and at times even unbearable. But remember God wastes nothing in our lives but will use it for His glory and our strength. Just be sure to share your redemptive story with others. I am!

Storms Versus Suffering

Notes

※ ※ ※

"I was never truly aware of my mother's brokenness. Whether it was due to her hiding it, or because my five-year-old self was more occupied with the love of my Barbie and Ken, either way, this perception of this time period fueled the already apparent idea of Black women needing to be a source of constant strength for her family. As I read this book, it gave me a new sense of freedom. A sense of freedom in being allowed to feel heartbroken and feel broken. While it presented a new (all-too-often), uncomfortable vulnerability, it also gave me a new sense of freedom in allowing myself to be a strong, Black women who can at times be very sad and lonely. A strong Black woman who occasionally needs to scream and cry in the car after a long day. Thank you, Mother, for showing your vulnerability, your authenticity, and your brokenness. While I've always respected your strength, I also now have the opportunity to respect your brokenness."

Salome Adelia
Fourth daughter
Doctoral Candidate
University of Missouri at Kansas City in
Clinical Psychology

※ ※ ※

Chapter Five

DIGGING UP DANDELIONS

A FRUSTRATING PART of brokenness is the repetition of destructive behaviors. Like being stuck in a rut, finding nothing to hold onto to pull yourself out, this is where I often found myself. I was repeating the same broken behaviors even after I prayed and promised with good intentions and heartfelt determination to never do them again. But Romans 7:19 rings so true: "For the good that I would I do not, but the evil which I would not, that I do" (KJV). I kept experiencing Band-aid fixes, and the Band-aids kept coming off.

I questioned God why I kept slipping back into broken places resulting in destructive behavior; back to behaviors I was trying my best not to do. God then took me back to one of my childhood experiences.

My father and I were in our front yard. I was playing, and my father was doing yard work. I asked him what he was doing, and he told me he was digging up dandelions (those yellow weeds that look like flowers). He was working pretty hard with each one. I could not understand why it was taking him so long and told him, "Daddy, all you got to do is rip off the yellow part, and it's all gone. See, no more dandelion!" as I snatched one up and held it in my hand for him to see. I remember my father chuckling and saying, "Sugar pie (that's what he called me), but it's not gone."

I said, "Yes, it is, Daddy, see?" as I showed him the yellow flower part in my hand.

"That's only the part that you see," he replied. "There is another part that is under the ground, and unless you get the root of that dandelion, it will come back again, growing another yellow flower part." My father had a garden tool that dug deep beneath the deceptive, flower-looking weed and ripped dandelions out by the root.

Part of mending brokenness is de-rooting the unwanted dandelions in our lives to make sure they won't come back. This means allowing God to take us back to the root or beginning place of our repetitive, destructive behaviors and rip our stuff up from the root from where they started. Because as good as my intentions were, I just kept ripping off the dandelion and trying to fix stuff with a Band-aid that would keep coming off, never getting to the root of where it all started.

When I go back to de-root in my life, I go back to unwanted, suppressed, or forgotten-about spaces (or closets) and expose or uncover raw areas, allowing God to heal, restore, and deliver. There were times I wanted to know where some of my jealousies, anger, hatred, attitudes, and bitterness roots originated, especially when they kept showing up. This is not a process for the faint-hearted because on some occasions, it meant I had to look at myself honestly (voice of vulnerability) and admit to the ugliness I saw. I had to discover and uncover errors, face insecurities, correct incorrect thought patterns, and discipline my mind from unholy distractions. Sometimes de-rooting took time because I denied, made excuses, or tried to justify why some of my dandelions were really flowers, not weeds. Sometimes it happened quickly. When our spirits are convicted, we ask for forgiveness, repent, and live in the power of Christ, not in our Band-aid fixes. It may be a journey to completion, but whatever it takes... trust God.

When I de-root, it takes me to the places where stuff first began in my life, so when those dandelions try to show up again, I understand the battle and realize where they are coming from. I can call them out, stand in my deliverance, and not follow the same pattern of thinking.

One de-rooting experience I had was the area of needing approval. I realized that some of my past behaviors were done simply so I could get approval from others. I was so deeply entrenched in it that I did not realize and found myself saying yes when I should have said no, because I wanted other people to accept me and think I was good enough.

So, I agreed to like things I did not like and do things I did not want to do. I said things I did not want to say and laughed at jokes I did not think were funny. I could have continued to live like this, because I had for many years, but I was not being true to myself or to God. People live false lives all the time. I had become comfortable in my discomfort.

The divorce painfully opened my spirit eyes to see this truth and sent me on a journey to find who I really was, who Christ created me to be. Don't get me wrong—I was not walking around like Ms. Jekyll and Ms. Hyde! Everything about my life was not horrible. But the divorce stripped me emotionally, leaving me raw. Everything I had leaned on, especially about myself, became rocky and unstable. I had become so engrossed in my roles as wife and mother that I had lost myself, who I was. This de-rooting was a cleansing experience and a little scary. It helped me see why and how I had become this way, and allowed me to unearth and renew my identity. The process took me back to my childhood, when I remembered constantly trying to prove to my family, I was as good as my brother. Now, no one told me that I was not as good, but I saw all the doting, attention, and pride around him. I wanted that too, and it became an endless battle trying to prove myself to gain approval. This desire and need spread to other areas and relationships in my life, and patterns of behavior were established.

Again, God did not leave me in this chasm of needing approval. He replaced that unclean spirit with Josh McDowell, an evangelical Christian apologist, evangelist, author and co-author's three points of "Seeing Myself as God Sees Me" [19]:

1) As eternally lovable: made in God's image

2) Infinitely valuable; I am "worth Jesus," to belong to Him

3) Thoroughly competent; God trusts me enough to leave me here to complete the ministry of reconciliation

De-rooting is more than just getting sins from their roots. It is also the healing and deliverance that we must replace our broken behaviors with. Please be reminded of Matthew 12:43-45, when the man was delivered from the unclean spirit, creating a new, empty, swept, and garnished place. And because nothing was put in the new, clean place, the same spirit returned with seven other unclean spirits; and the state of the man was worse than what he began with.

When we allow God to de-root, we must purposefully and deliberately receive His healing and deliverance. De-rooting takes our lives to new places and helps us understand why we behave and respond in certain ways. It is releasing and freeing because through the process, you begin to understand why and how things from the past continue to influence your present. Sometimes we realize we have always responded certain ways, and de-rooting helps us understand where and how we developed these patterns of responses. These may stem from childhood—protective, guarded responses a child would have. We must "grow up," however, and respond now as adults. Recognition is the first step of de-rooting. We need to ask God to help us uncover hidden or buried sins and must admit and confess our areas of insecurities, taking steps into memories, childhood, and the locked closets of our lives.

Does this sound scary or a part of suffering you would rather skip? God will never allow you to go where He will not make a way for you, and you will never go by yourself. He will walk with you through every memory or painful place, healing and delivering you as you go.

Mending Brokenness

<u>Notes</u>

"Inspiring...Encouraging...Healing...Transformative!!

Mending Brokenness describes a journey from despair to restoration. Have you ever been "-stuck in a rut-" and demonstrated "-destructive behaviors-". Well, *Mending Brokenness* describes what needs to be uprooted, detailing the descriptive process that's personally illustrated. It led me to reflect back more deeply into my own life's hurts, their impact, and my relationship with God. A vivid picture of hope in the struggle."

Joyce Simms-Tyson
Friend
Wisdom-bearer
Educator
Marital and Pre-marital Minister

Chapter Six

DANCING WITHOUT DADDY

THIS IS THE chapter I did not want to write, but it was one of my first broken places, and, at times, it still causes me emotional rawness. But now I am aware where that rawness comes from, so it does not pull me into a bottomless abyss. Before my de-rooting deliverance, I visited many abysses. Now I control where I go emotionally and how long I stay. My control came through my Christ-led deliverance. Before, I did not understand my dandelion emotions, and they took me everywhere anytime they felt like it. Broken periods are a part of our lives. They should not be ignored, pushed aside, denied, or forgotten: we should allow them to help us remember what we have learned and how we have grown.

I remember that night my daddy left and abandoned me. He and my mom stood by the front door in our dimly-lit living room. Daddy had his overcoat and brim hat on with his suitcase at his feet. I came in the room excited because when I saw the suitcase, I knew we must be going on a vacation. But my excitement quickly dissipated because I saw the look on both my parents' faces, and it was not excitement. I asked Daddy where he was going and if I could come with him. He said no, but that he would be back to visit me. But for an eight-year-old child, I asked myself why he had to visit when he lived here and why he had a suitcase when no one else did. Did it mean he would not be there in the morning when I woke up or at night when I went to bed? Would I still be his Sugar Pie? Did I do something to make him leave? So many questions. And because no one ever explained why Daddy had left, I lived life thinking problems were my fault, that I was the one who did something wrong. I found myself apologizing for things even when I was not at fault. I still unpack abandonment and self-blaming issues today, but I always remind myself to walk in my deliverance. Some behaviors we learn and practice over a lifetime. Walking in deliverance is a process with guaranteed success in Christ.

It was difficult to write this chapter because I love my daddy, Rufus T. Brown, so much. He was my dandelion guy. He made me feel special, and I was his Sugar Pie, but he left me when I needed him and was not a part of my life growing up. I needed him to reassure me that I was still his Sugar Pie when others, especially men, made me feel like mincemeat. I needed the security of my father being there every morning when I woke up and every evening when I went to bed.

Even after my parents divorced, we all still lived in the same city, and my parents still attended the same church. I remember the excruciating pain every Sunday as a child trying to decide where I was going to sit—with Mommy on the lower righthand side of the church or with Daddy on the rear left side on the Sundays they both did not usher. Daddy won most of the time because he had candy. Both parents told me I could sit with whoever I wanted to. I wanted to sit with them both because I loved both of them, but I had to choose.

Something I really wanted to do with Daddy, but never had a chance was a daddy/daughter dance with my little feet on top of his. I wanted us to dance together the way I had seen him and Mommy dance. Although we never danced together, I do believe I learned a different dance that I can do anytime and anywhere.

I do not regret any of my broken times. Of course, it is easier looking back and seeing them retrospectively. But if you are stuck in a quagmire of brokenness, don't quit or give up. It won't last forever, and it will work out for your good. Try to enjoy the dance and remember you either succeed or learn, and you are never by yourself. Someone needs to hear your story. It is your greatest asset.

Mending Brokenness

Notes

✹ ✹ ✹

"Most people will say their mother is what saved their life, but in my case it's actually true. Words cannot describe how much my mother has done not only for my siblings and I, but for so many kids in this world. My mother is such an ingrained part of my life; she has been my rock for so long. No one prepares for their life as they know it, to fall apart, but the strength she had to pick pieces up and start over (with five kids) is a testament to her fight and strength. My relationship with my mother has always been a deep and special one; it's something that I will always hold dear to my heart. I'm so grateful for a woman who used her brokenness to give her children space to truly be themselves, heal in the best ways they knew how and grieve deeply and wholeheartedly.

"Know that the legacy you built will always remain intact. You've done it mom; you've healed from brokenness and have so many examples to show that. I love you. I cherish you. The "great somebody's" have it from here."

Naomi Dorothy
Third daughter
Educational Consultant

✹ ✹ ✹

Chapter Seven

CONNECTING THE DOTS

I REMEMBER AS a child doing connect-the-dots pages in activity books. When I drew lines connecting the numbered dots, a picture or image became obvious. But until those lines we drawn, there were just a bunch of dots on a page. Connecting the dots can be a metaphor to illustrate the ability to associate one idea or event with another in order to find the big picture. But sometimes, there seems to be no big picture—just senseless, isolated, often painful "dots" of life. For me, my brokenness through the divorce, being vulnerable with God and myself, forgiving when I thought I had already forgiven, and other storms in my life were my dots. I saw no big picture; I saw no purpose and had no understanding. I tried to connect the dots of my brokenness, but could not because I needed God's perspective. I had to ask God what He wanted me to learn and how to see Him better.

When I asked Him to help me, He did and led me to 1 Peter 5:10, (KJV)-"But the God of all grace, who hath called us unto His eternal glory by Christ Jesus, after that ye have suffered a while, make you perfect, stablish, strengthen and settle you." That was my connecting line! After I had suffered for a while,

He would establish, strengthen, and settle me. It did not mean there would be no more "dots" or suffering in my life, but this word gave me the connectedness I was searching for; the assurance that God saw and understood me and my suffering and that through it, He would strengthen and settle me.

It did not explain or take away the pain of suffering, but God's Word did reassure me that it would not last forever and that through my suffering, I would get better and stronger. This was my new perspective.

I could understand better what Paul meant in 2 Corinthians 12:9 (KJV):

"And he said unto me, my grace is sufficient for thee, for my strength is made perfect in weakness. Most gladly [I am working on being glad] therefore will I rather glory in my infirmities that the power of Christ may rest upon me."

There will be dots in our lives—dots we understand, and dots we don't. But we must remember that our lives are not our own. When we give our lives to God, He gets to call the shots. We have been bought with a price, with the precious blood of Jesus. He knows what is best, and He wants the best for each of us. God does not just leave us out there in the "abyss of dots," bouncing off each one with no clue. As we yield our lives, past, present, and future to Him, not hiding or denying the truth about ourselves or our situations, God will help us unpack each dot, trusting that He has a plan for our lives (Jer. 29:11). Even when we cannot see or understand it or how and when our lives twist, turn and detour, it will STILL work out for our good (Rom. 8:28).

In our lives, we may have a bunch of dots, sometimes with unidentifiable connections. They may look jumbled and ungraspable, but God is our dot connector. He can make the dots of our lives into a picture that glorifies Him. Our life pictures may have some rough or ugly spots, or even some glitches, but a life full of dots yielded to God can create beauty out of what may seem like a mess. Part of mending is connecting the dots of our brokenness. We must ask and allow God to draw lines in our broken lives.

❄❄❄❄❄❄
<u>Notes</u>

"Words cannot express how admirable your strength is. They cannot express how much I appreciate and love you. I am continually in awe of the indelible love that was birthed through your brokenness and how that has morphed each of us into the people we are today. You are an example to so many of how God has the power to turn our ashes into beauty and our brokenness into strength.

Sarah Elizabeth
Second daughter
Boston Pubic School Teacher
Harvard University School of Education Graduate Student

Chapter Eight

START YOUR T.T.U. JOURNEY TODAY

THIS BOOK IS a testimonial intended to spark a fire in readers to pursue your God-led mending journeys. I describe my process in this book to show you that God has a journey of mending brokenness for you. It may be the same as mine (I doubt it), but I pray it isn't so God can grow and stretch you in different ways. What is your truth? Give it to God so He can make it right with His truth. The past cannot be changed, but it can be redeemed. Behind bitter experiences of the past, we can see God's providence. Psalm 34:18 (NIV) says, "God is so close to the broken-hearted and saves those who are crushed in spirit." Sound like you, where you are or have been? Let God begin or continue the process of mending, and trust Him through the journey. Here are some pearls of wisdom to leave with you.

The first pearl of wisdom is to trust God. An old adage that you have probably heard many times, but I encourage you every morning to wake up saying is, "Lord, I trust you." Richard Smallwood's song "Trust Me" [20] implores us to trust God. It starts off telling us that God will be with us and never leave us. This is what He promises to do, and the promise is there even before we trust. It continues to say that God will fight our battles if we will trust Him and allow Him to. God has all the power to deliver us. He knows life gets hard sometimes. He sees we are in the midst of a recession and a pandemic. But no matter what our circumstances look like, He promises to take care of us...if we trust Him.

Pearl of wisdom number two is that in our trusting, we have to believe He is turning things around for us. Vashawn Mitchell [21] starts his song, "Turning Around for Me", speaking to many of us. "Sometimes discouraged, but not defeated, cast down, but not destroyed" refers to 1 Cor 4:8-10, KJV. There are times we do not understand. I have definitely had struggles and disappointments and felt alone. But we must believe that God is turning things around for us. Make the proclamation, "God is mending me and turning it around for me. God is turning my brokenness into wholeness."

My husband preached a sermon about King Hezekiah, when Isaiah proclaimed that the king's life was about to end. After hearing this, Hezekiah turned toward the wall and prayed for his life to be extended. The point of his sermon was that Hezekiah turned toward the wall—with no place to go and no one he could turn to (Does that sound like a place of brokenness?)--- he turned away from everything and toward God. To mend brokenness, God is calling us to turn away from everything and everyone, and turn to Him—turn from and turn to. Believe and trust that it won't always be like this and that sooner or later, it will turn in your favor because God—not me, not you—is turning it around for you. We must trust and then turn.

The third pearl of wisdom: The Motor City Mass Choir sings a wonderful song titled "Use Me." [22] After we trust God to turn it around, we should humbly offer ourselves to be used by Him to manifest His glory. As unworthy as we are, He can and will use us. Offer yourself to Him as a living sacrifice (Rom 12:1) and come before Him, not as a spectator but as a participator in building His kingdom. God will use your story to add to His tapestry.

This is not a list of fifty steps or complicated readings, just three simple suggestions you can do daily: Trust, Turn, and be available to be Used—T. T. U. Trust whatever process God has for your journey and get excited that He has tailor-made a path just for you. Remember…God's got you. He promises to be with you and will never leave you. He will fight your battles. Continue to remember Colossians 1:29, (NASB) "For this purpose I also labor and strive according to His power which worketh mightily within me." His power is working mightily within you. Move out of the way, and watch Him turn your situation around and use you. To Him be all honor and glory and praise!

✻✻✻✻✻✻
<u>Notes</u>

Meditative Mending Questions

Journal your thoughts and answers, and then connect the dots! Ask God to show you His tapestry path to mending your brokenness.

1. What is your truth?

2. Are you broken now?

3. Have you been broken?

4. What is in your hidden closet?

5. Have your storms led to your brokenness?

6. What do you need to de-root?

7. Is there a sequence or series of things in your life you can connect to see a clearer picture of God's plan for you?

8. Do you have fear, shame, guilt, or denial that you can yield to God?

9. Are you ready and willing to go into your "ugly" places to receive deliverance and healing?

10. Once you have been delivered, what beauties will you put in place of those uglies?

Epilogue

GOOD NEWS

The hurtful family member and I continue to heal and build new bridges in our relationship, and communicate with continual forgiveness. Forgiveness continues to "sizzle" and sometimes shows up in situations I least expect. I am learning to love more through forgiveness.

KEEP READING

In the introduction, I mentioned there were five areas in my Kingdom Building Ministry. I only listed two in this publication—Train up a Child (opening my school) and writing this book. Please read future publications to learn about the other three.

BEST NEWS

To my children, Rachel Nicole, Sarah Elizabeth, Naomi Dorothy, Salome Adelia, and Alphonse Jireh—you have been with me through much of my brokenness, not always understanding it but always loving me through it. The many times I felt unlovable, you loved me. There were times we were broken together and helped each other, loving each other through each experience, which we still do. We also shared victories and blessings with each other. Thank you, and I love you even more.

To my Bonus-Children, Aaron Laurence, Kemba Renee, and Samantha Nicole—I came to you as a broken stepmom, and you loved and accepted me. I am grateful and love each of you.

YOUR NEWS

To readers: Allow your life to be a story and live a good one. Connect your dots, and weave your part of God's tapestry. Dance with your destiny, be vulnerable before God, keep peeling at your forgiveness, and de-root your brokenness dandelions. Then share your story with others so they can see what God can and will do. Remember that God does not waste anything that happens in your life. Allow Him to mend your brokenness and see the beauty He will make it because He is the Master Mender.

ADDITIONAL THANK-YOUS

To MY BIG brother, Reginald Thomas Brown: it has not always been easy, but I thank you for showing me how to keep pushing life's envelopes, even when you may be the only one pushing and to be a life-long learner. I have found my space and element, that you helped me to find and to be.

To Kemba Renee Gray-Ferguson thank you for the picture on the front of my first book. I am still in awe of all the wonderful gifts God has bestowed on you. Thank you for sharing them so freely. You are a "gifted gift" to me. Your mom, the late Christiana Renee, would be quite proud!

-KembasKreations2@gmail.com

To Lee Francois: Thank you for my author photo. Your gifts are astounding and abounding. You also have a book waiting to be birthed.

-www.fgstudios.net

To Michelle Denise Thomas-Monteiro: Thank you for writing the closing prayer. You are a prayer warrior, growing in God's grace. So proud of you as you trust Him more. Keep sharing your prayers!

To Sydney Janey, for your patience, passion and creativity designing my business logo.

sydney@sydneyjaneydesign.com

To C. B. Turner, my Bonus dad for loving my mother and her angel boy and angel girl.

To Barbara Ann Campbell, my Bonus sister, who loved me when I was not always lovable.

About the Author

Sabrina Fay Brown Gray, a native of Kansas City, Kansas, and a graduate of Wyandotte High School, moved to the Boston area to attend Brandeis University (BA) and Lesley College (MA). Sabrina's call is teaching and she has taught in various areas in the United States, in public, private, urban, and suburban locations. In 1988, she co-founded Cornerstone Christian Preparatory School. Sabrina is now retired after thirty-three years of teaching children, but continues to teach adults as an adjunct professor at Roxbury and Massbay Community Colleges.

Sabrina accepted the call to preach in 2005 and was ordained as an AME elder in 2008. She is a member of the Bethel AME ministerial staff where Ray Hammond and Gloria White-Hammond are her pastors. Her ministries have included being a Sunday school teacher, superintendent, and children's church director, and she currently serves as prayer ministry leader and coordinator for the Planning Ahead ministry. Sabrina has also traveled internationally and done missionary and educational work in Senegal and Tanzania. Her prayer is to return to Africa with her passion for teaching and preaching. She is currently the founder of Using Hands and Heart business and ministry, focusing on using her gifts of teaching, disciple-building, and mercy.

Sabrina ran her first marathon (26.2 miles) in Philadelphia at age sixty in 2016. She enjoys new challenges, reading, cooking, and running. Sabrina is the proud mother of five (Rachel, Sarah, Naomi, Salome, and Jireh), a grateful Bonus mom of three (Aaron, Kemba, and Samantha), an honored mother-in law to three, Kristin (Aaron), Damion (Kemba) and Nathaniel (Rachel) and a gallant grandmother of nine (currently): Kamran, Katherine, Lucille, Henry, Elizabeth, Ada, Josephine, Olivia and Theodore; with three grand dogs, Flint Tyrone, Luna, and CoCo Chanell and one grand cat, one-eye, Mike. She is the blessed wife of Rev. Robert Gray, assistant pastor of Bethel AME Church in Boston and Chaplain for the Boston Celtics. Sabrina is in love with Jesus and lives to worship, pray and serve Him, joyously waiting to see Jesus the Christ, face to face.

Closing Prayer

Dear Heavenly Father,

You knew from day one that Rev. Sabrina wanted to be an author from a very young age. It took many decades for her to put all her pain and heart break into words. She has been through trials and tribulation, from one storm after another, but through it all she came out on top with You. She did not let her pains ruin her life. Rev. Sabrina and Rev. Robert Gray, a good Christian man, have been together for two decades. It took her many trials and errors before she let go and let God. She was angry with You and in a dark place, but look at Rev. Sabrina and God now, they are best friends forever, for life. God, You, are so good and You will never leave us or forsake us. No matter what we are going through; Your light is always at the end of the tunnel. This too shall pass. Lord, help us to never, ever to forget this, no matter what the circumstances are in our lives. To God be the glory. In the name of Jesus, I say, Amen and amen! Blessings to all.

This prayer was written by Michelle Denise Thomas-Monteiro
Member of Bethel AME Church
Massachusetts Educator

Endnotes

1   Grant Faulkner, "Naked (on the page) and Afraid", Writer's Digest, July/August: 2015, Cincinnati, Ohio, 10.

2   Tim Gustafson, "I Can't Do It", Our Daily Bread, July 1, 2018, Volume 63, Numbers 3, 4, & 5, Grand Rapids, Michigan, 2018, 13.

3   Oswald Chambers, "Taking the Initiative Against Despair", My Utmost for His Highest, February 18, Discovery House Publishers. Grand Rapids, MI, 14.

4   Merriam-Webster Dictionary, http://www.merriam-webster.com/dictionary/mondegree,

5   Brene Brown, "Rising Strong", Random House, New York, 2015. 18.

6   Brene Brown, "Rising Strong", Random House, New York, 2015. 18.

7   Susan Nargala, Day 6-Devotion-Journeying with Jesus-40 Days Devotional-Bible.com, 2021, 19.

8   Dr. Wanda A. Turner, "Even With My Issues", Whitaker House, New Kensington, Pennsylvania, 1982, 19.

9   Victoria Osteen, "Love Your Life", Free Press, New York. London, Toronto, Sydney, 2008, 22.

10 Victoria Osteen, "Love Your Life", Free Press, New York, London, Toronto, Sydney, 2008, 22.

11 John Neider and Thomas M. Thompson, "Forgive and Love Again, Harvest House, Eugene, OR, 1991, 23.

12 Elizabeth Elliot, "A Path Through Suffering", Servant Publications, Ann Arbor, MI, 1990, 36.

13 Ruth Myers, "31 Days of Praise" Multnomah Publishers, Inc., Sisters, OR 1994, 26.

14 Yolanda Adams, "Through the Storm", 1991, Studio Album, trac 3, Through the Storm, Tribute Records, 1991, 26.

15 John Ogilvie, John, "Praying Trough the Tough Times", Harvest Hose Publishers, Eugene, Oregon, 1982, 26.

16 Ruth Myers, "31 Days of Praise" Multnomah Publishers, Inc., Sisters, OR 1994, 26.

17 Elizabeth Elliot, "A Path Through Suffering", Servant Publications, Ann Arbor, MI, 1990, 26.

Endnotes

18 "Footprints in the Sand", author unknown, 27.

19 Josh McDowell, "See Yourself as God Sees You", Tyndale House Publishing, Inc; Wheaton IL, 1999, 31.

20 Richard Smallwood, "Trust Me", 2011, Sony Legacy, Trac 14, Promises, 2011, 40.

21 Vashawn Mitchell, "Turning Around for Me", 2012, EMI Gospel, Trac 8, Created4This, 2012, 40.

22 Motor City Mass Choir, "Use Me", 1997, Integrity Music, Trac 4, Shout In the House, 1997, 41.

CPSIA information can be obtained
at www.ICGtesting.com
Printed in the USA
JSHW082226071122
32806JS00003B/190